Learn Python in One Day and Learn It Well

Python for Beginners with Hands-on Project

The only book you need to start coding in Python immediately

By Jamie Chan

http://www.learncodingfast.com/python

Preface

This book is written to help you learn Python programming FAST and learn it WELL. If you are an absolute beginner in Programming, you'll find that this book explains complex concepts in an easy to understand manner. Examples are carefully chosen to demonstrate each concept so that you can gain a deeper understand of the language. If you are an experienced coder, this book gives you a good base from which to explore Python. The appendices at the end of the book will also provide you with a convenient reference for some of the commonly used functions in Python.

In addition, as Richard Branson puts it: "The best way of learning about anything is by doing". At the end of the course, you'll be guided through a project that gives you a chance to put what you've learned to use.

You can download the source code for the project and the appendices at http://www.learncodingfast.com/python.

Table of Contents

Chapter 1: Python, what Python?

Welcome to the exciting world of programming. I'm so glad you picked up this book and I sincerely hope this book can help you master the Python language and experience the exhilaration of programming. Before we dive into the nuts and bolts of Python programming, let us first answer a few questions.

What is Python?

Python is a widely used high-level programming language created by Guido van Rossum in the late 1980s. The language places strong emphasis on code readability and simplicity, making it possible for programmers to develop applications rapidly.

Like all high level programming languages, Python code resembles the English language which computers are unable to understand. Codes that we write in Python have to be interpreted by a special program known as the Python interpreter, which we'll have to install before we can code, test and execute our Python programs. We'll look at how to install the Python interpreter in Chapter 2.

There are also a number of third-party tools, such as Py2exe or Pyinstaller that allow us to package our Python code into stand-alone executable programs for some of the most popular operating systems like Windows and Mac OS. This allows us to distribute our Python programs without requiring the users to install the Python interpreter.

Why Learn Python?

There are a large number of high level programming languages available, such as C, C++, and Java. The good news is all high level programming languages are very similar to one another. What differs is mainly the syntax, the libraries available and the way we access those libraries. A library is simply a collection of resources and pre-written codes that we can use when we write our programs. If you learn one language well, you can easily learn a new language in a fraction of the time it took you to learn the first language.

If you are new to programming, Python is a great place to start. One of the key features of Python is its simplicity, making it the ideal language for beginners to learn. Most programs in Python require considerably fewer lines of code to perform the same task compared to other languages such as C. This leads to fewer programming errors and reduces the development time needed. In addition, Python comes with an extensive collection of third party resources that extend the capabilities of the language. As such, Python can be used for a large variety of tasks, such as for desktop applications, database applications, network programming, game programming and even mobile development. Last but not least, Python is a cross platform language, which means that code written for one operating system, such as Windows, will work well on Mac OS or Linux without making any changes to the Python code.

Convinced that Python is THE language to learn? Let's get started...

Chapter 2: Getting ready for Python

Installing the Interpreter

Before we can write our first Python program, we have to download the appropriate interpreter for our computers.

We'll be using Python 3 in this book because as stated on the official Python site *"Python 2.x is legacy, Python 3.x is the present and future of the language"*. In addition, *"Python 3 eliminates many quirks that can unnecessarily trip up beginning programmers"*.

However, note that Python 2 is currently still rather widely used. Python 2 and 3 are about 90% similar. Hence if you learn Python 3, you will likely have no problems understanding codes written in Python 2.

To install the interpreter for Python 3, head over to https://www.python.org/downloads/. The correct version should be indicated at the top of the webpage. Click on the version for Python 3 and the software will start downloading.

Alternatively if you want to install a different version, scroll down the page and you'll see a listing of other versions. Click on the release version that you want. We'll be using version 3.4.2 in this book. You'll be redirected to the download page for that version.

x*y = 10

Division:
x/y = 2.5

Floor Division:
x//y = 2 (rounds down the answer to the nearest whole number)

Modulus:
x%y = 1 (gives the remainder when 5 is divided by 2)

Exponent:
x**y = 25 (5 to the power of 2)

More Assignment Operators

Besides the = sign, there are a few more assignment operators in Python (and most programming languages). These include operators like +=, -= and *=.

Suppose we have the variable x, with an initial value of 10. If we want to increment x by 2, we can write

```
x = x + 2
```

The program will first evaluate the expression on the right (x + 2) and assign the answer to the left. So eventually the statement above becomes x <- 12.

Instead of writing x = x + 2, we can also write x += 2 to express the same meaning. The += sign is actually a shorthand that combines the assignment sign with the addition operator. Hence, `x += 2` simply means `x = x + 2`.

Similarly, if we want to do a subtraction, we can write `x = x - 2` or `x -= 2`. The same works for all the 7 operators mentioned in the section above.

Chapter 4: Data Types in Python

In this chapter, we'll first look at some basic data types in Python, specifically the integer, float and string. Next, we'll explore the concept of type casting. Finally, we'll discuss three more advanced data types in Python: the list, tuple and dictionary.

Integers

Integers are numbers with no decimal parts, such as -5, -4, -3, 0, 5, 7 etc.

To declare an integer in Python, simply write
`variableName = initial value`

Example:
`userAge = 20, mobileNumber = 12398724`

Float

Float refers to numbers that have decimal parts, such as 1.234, -0.023, 12.01.

To declare a float in Python, we write `variableName = initial value`

Example:
`userHeight = 1.82, userWeight = 67.2`

String

String refers to text.

To declare a string, you can either use `variableName = 'initial value'` (single quotes) or `variableName = "initial value"` (double quotes)

Example:
`userName = 'Peter'`, `userSpouseName = "Janet"`, `userAge = '30'`

In the last example, because we wrote `userAge = '30'`, `userAge` is a string. In contrast, if you wrote `userAge = 30` (without quotes), `userAge` is an integer.

We can combine multiple substrings by using the concatenate sign (+). For instance, `"Peter" + "Lee"` is equivalent to the string `"PeterLee"`.

Built-In String Functions

Python includes a number of built-in functions to manipulate strings. A function is simply a block of reusable code that performs a certain task. We'll discuss functions in greater depth in Chapter 7.

An example of a function available in Python is the `upper()` method for strings. You use it to capitalize all the letters in a string. For instance, `'Peter'.upper()` will give us the string `"PETER"`. You can refer to Appendix A for more examples and sample codes on how to use Python's built-in string methods.

Formatting Strings using the % Operator

Strings can also be formatted using the % operator. This

gives you greater control over how you want your string to be displayed and stored. The syntax for using the % operator is

```
"string to be formatted" %(values or
variables to be inserted into string,
separated by commas)
```

There are three parts to this syntax. First we write the string to be formatted in quotes. Next we write the % symbol. Finally, we have a pair of round brackets ( ) within which we write the values or variables to be inserted into the string. This round brackets with values inside is actually known as a tuple, a data type that we'll cover in the chapter later.

Type the following code in IDLE and run it.

```
brand = 'Apple'
exchangeRate = 1.235235245

message = 'The price of this %s laptop is
%d USD and the exchange rate is %4.2f USD
to 1 EUR' %(brand, 1299, exchangeRate)

print (message)
```

In the example above, the string `'The price of this %s laptop is %d USD and the exchange rate is %4.2f USD to 1 EUR'` is the string that we want to format. We use the `%s`, `%d` and `%4.2f` formatters as placeholders in the string.

These placeholders will be replaced with the variable `brand`, the value 1299 and the variable `exchangeRate` respectively, as indicated in the round brackets. If we run the code, we'll get the output below.

```
The price of this Apple laptop is 1299 USD
and the exchange rate is 1.24 USD to 1 EUR
```

The `%s` formatter is used to represent a string ("Apple" in this case) while the `%d` formatter represents an integer (1299). If we want to add spaces before an integer, we can add a number between `%` and `d` to indicate the desired length of the string. For instance `"%5d" % (123)` will give us `"  123"` (with 2 spaces in front and a total length of 5).

The %f formatter is used to format floats (numbers with decimals). Here we format it as %4.2f where 4 refers to the total length and 2 refers to 2 decimal places. If we want to add spaces before the number, we can format is as %7.2f, which will give us `"   1.24"` (with 2 decimal places, 3 spaces in front and a total length of 7).

Formatting Strings using the `format()` method

In addition to using the % operator to format strings, Python also provides us with the `format()` method to format strings. The syntax is

```
"string to be formatted".format(values or
variables to be inserted into string,
separated by commas)
```

When we use the format method, we do not use `%s`, `%f` or

Example:
```
userAge = [21, 22, 23, 24, 25]
```

We can also declare a list without assigning any initial values to it. We simply write `listName = []`. What we have now is an empty list with no items in it. We have to use the `append()` method mentioned below to add items to the list.

Individual values in the list are accessible by their indexes, and indexes always start from ZERO, not 1. This is a common practice in almost all programming languages, such as C and Java. Hence the first value has an index of 0, the next has an index of 1 and so forth. For instance, `userAge[0] = 21`, `userAge[1] = 22`

Alternatively, you can access the values of a list from the back. The last item in the list has an index of -1, the second last has an index of -2 and so forth. Hence, `userAge[-1] = 25`, `userAge[-2] = 24`.

You can assign a list, or part of it, to a variable. If you write `userAge2 = userAge`, the variable `userAge2` becomes `[21, 22, 23, 24, 25]`.

If you write `userAge3 = userAge[2:4]`, you are assigning items with index 2 to index 4-1 from the list `userAge` to the list `userAge3`. In other words, `userAge3 = [23, 24]`.
The notation 2:4 is known as a slice. Whenever we use the slice notation in Python, the item at the start index is always included, but <u>the item at the end is always excluded</u>. Hence the notation 2:4 refers to items from index

2 to index 4-1 (i.e. index 3), which is why `userAge3` = `[23, 24]` and not `[23, 24, 25]`.

The slice notation includes a third number known as the stepper. If we write `userAge4 = userAge[1:5:2]`, we will get a sub list consisting of <u>every second number</u> from index 1 to index 5-1 because the stepper is 2. Hence, `userAge4 = [22, 24]`.

In addition, slice notations have useful defaults. The default for the first number is zero, and the default for the second number is size of the list being sliced. For instance, `userAge[ :4]` gives you values from index 0 to index 4-1 while `userAge[1: ]` gives you values from index 1 to index 5-1 (since the size of `userAge` is 5, i.e. `userAge` has 5 items).

To modify items in a list, we write `listName[index of item to be modified] = new value`. For instance, if you want to modify the second item, you write `userAge[1] = 5`. Your list becomes `userAge = [21, 5, 23, 24, 25]`

To add items, you use the `append()` function. For instance, if you write `userAge.append(99)`, you add the value 99 to the end of the list. Your list is now `userAge = [21, 5, 23, 24, 25, 99]`

To remove items, you write `del listName[index of item to be deleted]`. For instance, if you write `del userAge[2]`, your list now becomes `userAge = [21, 5, 24, 25, 99]` (the third item is deleted)

To fully appreciate the workings of a list, try running the following program.

```
#declaring the list, list elements can be
of different data types
myList = [1, 2, 3, 4, 5, "Hello"]

#print the entire list.
print(myList)
#You'll get [1, 2, 3, 4, 5, "Hello"]

#print the third item (recall: Index starts
from zero).
print(myList[2])
#You'll get 3

#print the last item.
print(myList[-1])
#You'll get "Hello"

#assign myList (from index 1 to 4) to
myList2 and print myList2
myList2 = myList[1:5]
print (myList2)
#You'll get [2, 3, 4, 5]

#modify the second item in myList and print
the updated list
myList[1] = 20
print(myList)
#You'll get [1, 20, 3, 4, 5, 'Hello']
#append a new item to myList and print the
updated list
myList.append("How are you")
```

```
print(myList)
#You'll get [1, 20, 3, 4, 5, 'Hello', 'How
are you']
#remove the sixth item from myList and
print the updated list
del myList[5]
print(myList)
#You'll get [1, 20, 3, 4, 5, 'How are you']
```

There are a couple more things that you can do with a list. For sample codes and more examples on working with a list, refer to Appendix B.

Tuple

Tuples are just like lists, but you cannot modify their values. The initial values are the values that will stay for the rest of the program. An example where tuples are useful is when your program needs to store the names of the months of the year.

To declare a tuple, you write `tupleName = (initial values)`. Notice that we use round brackets ( ) when declaring a tuple. Multiple values are separated by a comma.

Example:
```
monthsOfYear = ("Jan", "Feb", "Mar", "Apr",
"May", "Jun", "Jul", "Aug", "Sep", "Oct",
"Nov", "Dec")
```

You access the individual values of a tuple using their indexes, just like with a list.

Hence, `monthsOfYear[0] = "Jan"`,
`monthsOfYear[-1] = "Dec"`.

For more examples of what you can do with a tuple, check out Appendix C.

Dictionary

Dictionary is a collection of related data PAIRS. For instance, if we want to store the username and age of 5 users, we can store them in a dictionary.

To declare a dictionary, you write `dictionaryName = {dictionary key : data}`, with the requirement that dictionary keys must be unique (within one dictionary). That is, you cannot declare a dictionary like this `myDictionary = {"Peter":38, "John":51, "Peter":13}`.

This is because "Peter" is used as the dictionary key twice. Note that we use curly brackets { } when declaring a dictionary. Multiple pairs are separated by a comma.

Example:
`userNameAndAge = {"Peter":38, "John":51, "Alex":13, "Alvin":"Not Available"}`

You can also declare a dictionary using the `dict( )` method. To declare the `userNameAndAge` dictionary above, you write

`userNameAndAge = dict(Peter = 38, John = 51, Alex = 13, Alvin = "Not Available")`

When you use this method to declare a dictionary, you use round brackets ( ) instead of curly brackets { } and you do not put quotation marks for the dictionary keys.

To access individual items in the dictionary, we use the dictionary key, which is the first value in the {dictionary key : data} pair. For instance, to get John's age, you write userNameAndAge["John"]. You'll get the value 51.

To modify items in a dictionary, we write dictionaryName[dictionary key of item to be modified] = new data. For instance, to modify the "John":51 pair, we write userNameAndAge["John"] = 21. Our dictionary now becomes userNameAndAge = {"Peter":38, "John":21, "Alex":13, "Alvin":"Not Available"}.

We can also declare a dictionary without assigning any initial values to it. We simply write dictionaryName = { }. What we have now is an empty dictionary with no items in it.

To add items to a dictionary, we write dictionaryName[dictionary key] = data. For instance, if we want to add "Joe":40 to our dictionary, we write userNameAndAge["Joe"] = 40. Our dictionary now becomes userNameAndAge = {"Peter":38, "John":21, "Alex":13, "Alvin":"Not Available", "Joe":40}

To remove items from a dictionary, we write del dictionaryName[dictionary key]. For instance, to remove the "Alex":13 pair, we write del

userNameAndAge["Alex"]. Our dictionary now
becomes userNameAndAge = {"Peter":38,
"John":21, "Alvin":"Not Available",
"Joe":40}

Run the following program to see all these in action.

```
#declaring the dictionary, dictionary keys
and data can be of different data types
myDict = {"One":1.35, 2.5:"Two Point Five",
3:"+", 7.9:2}

#print the entire dictionary
print(myDict)
#You'll get {2.5: 'Two Point Five', 3: '+',
'One': 1.35, 7.9: 2}
#Note that items in a dictionary are not
stored in the same order as the way you
declare them.

#print the item with key = "One".
print(myDict["One"])
#You'll get 1.35

#print the item with key = 7.9.
print(myDict[7.9])
#You'll get 2

#modify the item with key = 2.5 and print
the updated dictionary
myDict[2.5] = "Two and a Half"
print(myDict)
#You'll get {2.5: 'Two and a Half', 3: '+',
'One': 1.35, 7.9: 2}
```

```
#add a new item and print the updated
dictionary
myDict["New item"] = "I'm new"
print(myDict)
#You'll get {'New item': 'I'm new', 2.5:
'Two and a Half', 3: '+', 'One': 1.35, 7.9:
2}

#remove the item with key = "One" and print
the updated dictionary
del myDict["One"]
print(myDict)
#You'll get {'New item': 'I'm new', 2.5:
'Two and a Half', 3: '+', 7.9: 2}
```

For more examples and sample codes of working with a dictionary, you can refer to Appendix D.

Chapter 5: Making Your Program Interactive

Now that we've covered the basics of variables, let us write a program that makes use of them. We'll revisit the "Hello World" program we wrote in Chapter 2, but this time we'll make it interactive. Instead of just saying hello to the world, we want the world to know our names and ages too. In order to do that, our program needs to be able to prompt us for information and display them on the screen.

Two built-in functions can do that for us: `input()` and `print()`.

For now, let's type the following program in IDLE. Save it and run it.

```
myName = input("Please enter your name: ")
myAge = input("What about your age: ")

print ("Hello World, my name is", myName,
"and I am", myAge, "years old.")
```

The program should prompt you for your name.

```
Please enter your name:
```

Supposed you entered James. Now press Enter and it'll prompt you for your age.

```
What about your age:
```

Say you keyed in 20. Now press Enter again. You should get the following statement:

```
Hello World, my name is James and I am 20
years old.
```

Input()

In the example above, we used the `input()` function twice to get our user's name and age.

```
myName = input("Please enter your name: ")
```

The string "Please enter your name: " is the prompt that will be displayed on the screen to give instructions to the user. After the user enters the relevant information, this information is stored **as a string** in the variable `myName`. The next input statement prompts the user for his age and stores the information **as a string** in the variable `myAge`.

The `input()` function differs slightly in Python 2 and Python 3. In Python 2, if you want to accept user input as a string, you have to use the `raw_input()` function instead.

Print()

The `print()` function is used to display information to users. It accepts zero or more expressions as parameters, separated by commas.

In the statement below, we passed 5 parameters to the `print()` function. Can you identify them?

```
print ("Hello World, my name is", myName,
"and I am", myAge, "years old.")
```
The first is the string "Hello World, my name is"
The next is the variable myName declared using the input
function earlier.
Next is the string "and I am", followed by the variable
myAge and finally the string "years old.".

Note that we do not use quotation marks when referring to
the variables myName and myAge. If you use quotation
marks, you'll get the output

```
Hello World, my name is myName and I am
myAge years old.
```

instead, which is obviously not what we want.

Another way to print a statement with variables is to use
the % formatter we learned in Chapter 4. To achieve the
same output as the first print statement above, we can
write

```
print ("Hello World, my name is %s and I am
%s years old." %(myName, myAge))
```

Finally, to print the same statement using the format()
method, we write

```
print ("Hello World, my name is {} and I am
{} years old".format(myName, myAge))
```

The print() function is another function that differs in
Python 2 and Python 3. In Python 2, you'll write it without

brackets, like this:

```
print "Hello World, my name is " + myName +
" and I am " + myAge + " years old."
```

Triple Quotes

If you need to display a long message, you can use the triple-quote symbol (''' or """) to span your message over multiple lines. For instance,

```
print ('''Hello World.
My name is James and
I am 20 years old.''')
```

will give you

```
Hello World.
My name is James and
I am 20 years old.
```

This helps to increase the readability of your message.

Escape Characters

Sometimes we may need to print some special "unprintable" characters such as a tab or a newline. In this case, you need to use the \ (backslash) character to escape characters that otherwise have a different meaning.

For instance to print a tab, we type the backslash character before the letter t, like this: \t. Without the \ character, the letter t will be printed. With it, a tab is printed. Hence, if you type `print ('Hello\tWorld')`, you'll get `Hello World`

Other common uses of the backslash character are shown below.
`>>>` shows the command and the following lines show the output.

\n (Prints a newline)

```
>>> print ('Hello\nWorld')
Hello
World
```

\\ (Prints the backslash character itself)

```
>>> print ('\\')
\
```

\" (Prints double quote, so that the double quote does not signal the end of the string)

```
>>> print ("I am 5'9\" tall")
I am 5'9" tall
```

\' (Print single quote, so that the single quote does not signal the end of the string)

```
>>> print ('I am 5\'9" tall')
I am 5'9" tall
```

If you do not want characters preceded by the \ character to be interpreted as special characters, you can use raw strings by adding an r before the first quote. For instance, if you do not want \t to be interpreted as a tab, you should type `print (r'Hello\tWorld')`. You will get `Hello\tWorld` as the output.

Chapter 6: Making Choices and Decisions

Congratulations, you've made it to the most interesting chapter. I hope you've enjoyed the course so far. In this chapter, we'll look at how to make your program smarter, capable of making choices and decisions. Specifically, we'll be looking at the `if` statement, `for` loop and `while` loop. These are known as control flow tools; they control the flow of the program. In addition, we'll also look at the `try, except` statement that determines what the program should do when an error occurs.

However, before we go into these control flow tools, we have to first look at condition statements.

Condition Statements

All control flow tools involve evaluating a condition statement. The program will proceed differently depending on whether the condition is met.

The most common condition statement is the comparison statement. If we want to compare whether two variables are the same, we use the == sign (double =). For instance, if you write $x == y$, you are asking the program to check if the value of x is equals to the value of y. If they are equal, the condition is met and the statement will evaluate to `True`. Else, the statement will evaluate to `False`.

Other comparison signs include != (not equals), < (smaller than), > (greater than), <= (smaller than or equals to) and >= (greater than or equals to). The list below shows how these signs can be used and gives examples of statements that will evaluate to `True`.

Not equals:
5 != 2

Greater than:
5>2

Smaller than:
2<5

Greater than or equals to:
5>=2
5>=5

Smaller than or equals to:
2 <= 5
2 <= 2

We also have three logical operators, `and`, `or`, `not` that are useful if we want to combine multiple conditions.

The `and` operator returns `True` if all conditions are met. Else it will return `False`. For instance, the statement `5==5 and 2>1` will return `True` since both conditions are `True`.

The `or` operator returns `True` if <u>at least one</u> condition is met. Else it will return `False`. The statement `5 > 2 or 7 > 10 or 3 == 2` will return `True` since the first condition `5>2` is `True`.

The `not` operator returns `True` if the condition after the `not` keyword is false. Else it will return `False`. The statement `not 2>5` will return `True` since 2 is not greater than 5.

If Statement

The `if` statement is one of the most commonly used control flow statements. It allows the program to evaluate if a certain condition is met, and to perform the appropriate action based on the result of the evaluation. The structure of an `if` statement is as follows:

```
if condition 1 is met:
     do A
elif condition 2 is met:
     do B
elif condition 3 is met:
     do C
elif condition 4 is met:
     do D
else:
     do E
```

`elif` stands for "else if" and you can have as many `elif` statements as you like.

If you've coded in other languages like C or Java before, you may be surprised to notice that no parentheses ( ) are needed in Python after the `if`, `elif` and `else` keyword. In addition, Python does not use curly { } brackets to define the start and end of the `if` statement. Rather, Python uses indentation. Anything indented is treated as a block of code that will be executed if the condition evaluates to true.

To fully understand how the `if` statement works, fire up IDLE and key in the following code.

```
userInput = input('Enter 1 or 2: ')

if userInput == "1":
        print ("Hello World")
        print ("How are you?")
elif userInput == "2":
        print ("Python Rocks!")
        print ("I love Python")
else:
        print ("You did not enter a valid
number")
```

The program first prompts the user for an input using the `input` function. The result is stored in the `userInput` variable as a string.

Next the statement `if userInput == "1":` compares the `userInput` variable with the string "1". If the value stored in `userInput` is "1", the program will execute all statements that are indented until the indentation ends. In this example, it'll print "`Hello World`", followed by "`How are you?`".

Alternatively, if the value stored in `userInput` is "2", the program will print "`Python Rocks`", followed by "`I love Python`".

For all other values, the program will print "You did not enter a valid number".

Run the program three times, enter 1, 2 and 3 respectively for each run. You'll get the following output:

```
Enter 1 or 2: 1
Hello World
How are you?

Enter 1 or 2: 2
Python Rocks!
I love Python

Enter 1 or 2: 3
You did not enter a valid number
```

Inline If

An inline if statement is a simpler form of an if statement and is more convenient if you only need to perform a simple task. The syntax is:

```
do Task A if condition is true else do Task
B
```

For instance,

```
num1 = 12 if myInt==10 else 13
```

This statement assigns 12 to num1 (Task A) if myInt equals to 10. Else it assigns 13 to num1 (Task B).

Another example is

```
print ("This is task A" if myInt == 10 else
"This is task B")
```

This statement prints `"This is task A"` (Task A) if `myInt` equals to 10. Else it prints `"This is task B"` (Task B).

For Loop

Next, let us look at the `for` loop. The `for` loop executes a block of code repeatedly until the condition in the `for` statement is no longer valid.

Looping through an iterable

In Python, an iterable refers to anything that can be looped over, such as a string, list or tuple. The syntax for looping through an iterable is as follows:

```
for a in iterable:
     print (a)
```

Example:

```
pets = ['cats', 'dogs', 'rabbits',
'hamsters']

for myPets in pets:
     print (myPets)
```

In the program above, we first declare the list `pets` and give it the members `'cats'`, `'dogs'`, `'rabbits'` and `'hamsters'`. Next the statement `for myPets in` `pets:` loops through the `pets` list and assigns each member in the list to the variable `myPets`.

The first time the program runs through the `for` loop, it assigns 'cats' to the variable `myPets`. The statement `print (myPets)` then prints the value 'cats'. The second time the programs loops through the `for` statement, it assigns the value 'dogs' to `myPets` and prints the value 'dogs'. The program continues looping through the list until the end of the list is reached.

If you run the program, you'll get

```
cats
dogs
rabbits
hamsters
```

We can also display the index of the members in the list. To do that, we use the `enumerate()` function.

```
for index, myPets in enumerate(pets):
      print (index, myPets)
```

This will give us the output

```
0 cats
1 dogs
2 rabbits
3 hamster
```

The next example shows how to loop through a string.

```
message = 'Hello'
```

```
for i in message:
        print (i)
```

The output is

```
H
e
l
l
o
```

Looping through a sequence of numbers

To loop through a sequence of numbers, the built-in `range()` function comes in handy. The `range()` function generates a list of numbers and has the syntax `range (start, end, step)`.

If `start` is not given, the numbers generated will start from zero.

Note: A useful tip to remember here is that in Python (and most programming languages), unless otherwise stated, we always start from zero.

For instance, the index of a list and a tuple starts from zero.
When using the `format()` method for strings, the positions of parameters start from zero.
When using the `range()` function, if `start` is not given, the numbers generated start from zero.

If `step` is not given, a list of consecutive numbers will be generated (i.e. step = 1). The `end` value must be provided. However, one weird thing about the `range ()` function is that the given `end` value is never part of the generated list.

For instance,
`range (5)` will generate the list [0, 1, 2, 3, 4]
`range (3, 10)` will generate [3, 4, 5, 6, 7, 8, 9]
`range (4, 10, 2)` will generate [4, 6, 8]

To see how the `range ()` function works in a `for` statement, try running the following code:

```
for i in range (5) :
     print (i)
```

You should get
```
0
1
2
3
4
```

While Loop

The next control flow statement we are going to look at is the `while` loop. Like the name suggests, a `while` loop repeatedly executes instructions inside the loop while a certain condition remains valid. The structure of a `while` statement is as follows:

```
while condition is true:
     do A
```

Most of the time when using a `while` loop, we need to first declare a variable to function as a loop counter. Let's just call this variable `counter`. The condition in the `while` statement will evaluate the value of `counter` to determine if it smaller (or greater) than a certain value. If it is, the loop will be executed. Let's look at a sample program.

```
counter = 5

while counter > 0:
        print ("Counter = ", counter)
        counter = counter - 1
```

If you run the program, you'll get the following output

```
Counter = 5
Counter = 4
Counter = 3
Counter = 2
Counter = 1
```

At first look, a `while` statement seems to have the simplest syntax and should be the easiest to use. However, one has to be careful when using `while` loops due to the danger of infinite loops. Notice that in the program above, we have the line `counter = counter - 1`? This line is crucial. It decreases the value of `counter` by 1 and assigns this new value back to `counter`, overwriting the original value.

We need to decrease the value of `counter` by 1 so that the loop condition `while counter > 0` will eventually evaluate to `False`. If we forget to do that, the loop will keep running endlessly resulting in an infinite loop. If you want to experience this first hand, just delete the line `counter = counter - 1` and try running the program again. The program will keep printing `counter = 5` until you somehow kill the program. Not a pleasant experience especially if you have a large program and you have no idea which code segment is causing the infinite loop.

Break

When working with loops, sometimes you may want to exit the entire loop when a certain condition is met. To do that, we use the `break` keyword. Run the following program to see how it works.

```
j = 0
for i in range(5):
    j = j + 2
    print ('i = ', i, ', j = ', j)
    if j == 6:
        break
```

You should get the following output.

```
i =  0 , j =  2
i =  1 , j =  4
i =  2 , j =  6
```

Without the `break` keyword, the program should loop from i = 0 to i = 4 because we used the function `range(5)`. However with the `break` keyword, the program ends prematurely at i = 2. This is because when i = 2, j reaches the value of 6 and the `break` keyword causes the loop to end.

In the example above, notice that we used an `if` statement within a `for` loop. It is very common for us to 'mix-and-match' various control tools in programming, such as using a `while` loop inside an `if` statement or using a `for` loop inside a `while` loop. This is known as a nested control statement.

Continue

Another useful keyword for loops is the `continue` keyword. When we use `continue`, the rest of the loop after the keyword is skipped for that iteration. An example will make it clearer.

```
j = 0
for i in range(5):
        j = j + 2
        print ('\ni = ', i, ', j = ', j)
        if j == 6:
                continue
        print ('I will be skipped over if
j=6')
```

You will get the following output:

```
i =  0 , j =  2
I will be skipped over if j=6

i =  1 , j =  4
I will be skipped over if j=6

i =  2 , j =  6
```

```
i =   3 , j =   8
I will be skipped over if j=6

i =   4 , j =   10
I will be skipped over if j=6
```

When j = 6, the line after the `continue` keyword is not printed. Other than that, everything runs as per normal.

Try, Except

The final control statement we'll look at is the `try,` `except` statement. This statement controls how the program proceeds when an error occurs. The syntax is as follows:

```
try:
      do something
except:
      do something else when an error occurs
```

For instance, try running the program below

```
try:
      answer =12/0
      print (answer)
except:
      print ("An error occurred")
```

When you run the program, you'll get the message "An error occurred". This is because when the program tries to execute the statement `answer =12/0` in the `try` block, an error occurs since you cannot divide a number by zero. The remaining of the `try` block is ignored and the statement in the `except` block is executed instead.

If you want to display more specific error messages to your users depending on the error, you can specify the error type after the `except` keyword. Try running the program below.

```
try:
    userInput1 = int(input("Please enter a number: "))
    userInput2 = int(input("Please enter another number: "))
    answer =userInput1/userInput2
    print ("The answer is ", answer)
    myFile = open("missing.txt", 'r')
except ValueError:
    print ("Error: You did not enter a number")
except ZeroDivisionError:
    print ("Error: Cannot divide by zero")
except Exception as e:
    print ("Unknown error: ", e)
```

The list below shows the various outputs for different user inputs. >>> denotes the user input and => denotes the output.

```
>>> Please enter a number: m
=> Error: You did not enter a number
```

Reason: User entered a string which cannot be cast into an integer. This is a `ValueError`. Hence, the statement in the `except ValueError` block is displayed.

```
>>> Please enter a number: 12
>>> Please enter another number: 0
=> Error: Cannot divide by zero
```

Reason: `userInput2` = 0. Since we cannot divide a number by zero, this is a `ZeroDivisionError`. The statement in the `except ZeroDivisionError` block is displayed.

```
>>> Please enter a number: 12
>>> Please enter another number: 3
=> The answer is   4.0
=> Unknown error:   [Errno 2] No such file
or directory: 'missing.txt'
```

Reason: User enters acceptable values and the line `print ("The answer is ", answer)` executes correctly. However, the next line raises an error as missing.txt is not found. Since this is not a `ValueError` or a `ZeroDivisionError`, the last `except` block is executed.

`ValueError` and `ZeroDivisionError` are two of the many pre-defined error types in Python. `ValueError` is raised when a built-in operation or function receives a parameter that has the right type but an inappropriate value. `ZeroDivisionError` is raised when the program tries to divide by zero. Other common errors in Python include

IOError:
Raised when an I/O operation (such as the built-in `open ()` function) fails for an I/O-related reason, e.g., "file not found".

ImportError:
Raised when an import statement fails to find the module definition

IndexError:
Raised when a sequence (e.g. string, list, tuple) index is out of range.

KeyError:
Raised when a dictionary key is not found.

NameError:
Raised when a local or global name is not found.

TypeError:
Raised when an operation or function is applied to an object of inappropriate type.

For a complete list of all the error types in Python, you can refer to https://docs.python.org/3/library/exceptions.html.

Python also comes with pre-defined error messages for each of the different types of errors. If you want to display the message, you use the `as` keyword after the error type. For instance, to display the default `ValueError` message, you write:

```
except ValueError as e:
    print (e)
```

`e` is the variable name assigned to the error. You can give it some other names, but it is common practice to use `e`. The last except statement in our program

```
except Exception as e:
        print ("Unknown error: ", e)
```

is an example of using the pre-defined error message. It
serves as a final attempt to catch any unanticipated errors.

Chapter 7: Functions and Modules

In our previous chapters, we've briefly mentioned functions and modules. In this chapter, let's look at them in detail. To reiterate, all programming languages come with built-in codes that we can use to make our lives easier as programmers. These codes consist of pre-written classes, variables and functions for performing certain common tasks and are saved in files known as modules. Let's first look at functions.

What are Functions?

Functions are simply pre-written codes that perform a certain task. For an analogy, think of the mathematical functions available in MS Excel. To add numbers, we can use the sum() function and type sum(A1:A5) instead of typing A1+A2+A3+A4+A5.

Depending on how the function is written, whether it is part of a class (a class is a concept in object-oriented programming which we will not cover in this book) and how you import it, we can call a function simply by typing the name of the function or by using the dot notation. Some functions require us to pass data in for them to perform their tasks. These data are known as parameters and we pass them to the function by enclosing their values in parenthesis ( ) separated by commas.

For instance, to use the `print()` function for displaying text on the screen, we call it by typing `print("Hello World")` where `print` is the name of the function and `"Hello World"` is the parameter.

On the other hand, to use the `replace()` function for manipulating text strings, we have to type "`Hello World`".`replace`("`World`", "`Universe`") where `replace` is the name of the function and "`World`" and "`Universe`" are the parameters. The string before the dot (i.e. "`Hello World`") is the string that will be affected. Hence, "`Hello World`" will be changed to "`Hello Universe`".

Defining Your Own Functions

We can define our own functions in Python and reuse them throughout the program. The syntax for defining a function is as follows:

```
def functionName(parameters):
      code detailing what the function
should do
      return [expression]
```

There are two keywords here, `def` and `return`.

`def` tells the program that the indented code from the next line onwards is part of the function. `return` is the keyword that we use to return an answer from the function. There can be more than one `return` statements in a function. However, once the function executes a `return` statement, the function will exit. If your function does not need to return any value, you can omit the `return` statement. Alternatively, you can write `return` or `return None`.

Let us now define our first function. Suppose we want to determine if a given number is a prime number. Here's how we can define the function using the modulus (%) operator we learned in Chapter 3 and the `for` loop and `if` statement we learned in Chapter 6.

```
def checkIfPrime (numberToCheck):
    for x in range(2, numberToCheck):
        if (numberToCheck%x == 0):
            return False
    return True
```

In the function above, lines 2 and 3 uses a `for` loop to divide the given parameter `numberToCheck` by all numbers from 2 to `numberToCheck` - 1 to determine if the remainder is zero. If the remainder is zero, `numberToCheck` is not a prime number. Line 4 will return `False` and the function will exit.

If by last iteration of the `for` loop, none of the division gives a remainder of zero, the function will reach Line 5, and return `True`. The function will then exit.

To use this function, we type `checkIfPrime (13)` and assign it to a variable like this

```
answer = checkIfPrime (13)
```

Here we are passing in 13 as the parameter. We can then print the answer by typing `print (answer)`. We'll get the output: `True`.

Variable Scope

An important concept to understand when defining a function is the concept of variable scope. Variables defined inside a function are treated differently from variables defined outside. There are two main differences.

Firstly, any variable declared <u>inside</u> a function is only accessible within the function. These are known as local variables. Any variable declared outside a function is known as a global variable and is accessible anywhere in the program.

To understand this, try the code below:

```
message1 = "Global Variable"

def myFunction():
      print("\nINSIDE THE FUNCTION")
      #Global variables are accessible
inside a function
      print (message1)
      #Declaring a local variable
      message2 = "Local Variable"
      print (message2)

#Calling the function
myFunction()

print("\nOUTSIDE THE FUNCTION")

#Global variables are accessible outside
function
print (message1)

#Local variables are NOT accessible outside
function.
print (message2)
```

If you run the program, you will get the output below.

```
INSIDE THE FUNCTION
Global Variable
Local Variable

OUTSIDE THE FUNCTION
Global Variable
NameError: name 'message2' is not defined
```

Within the function, both the local and global variables are accessible. Outside the function, the local variable `message2` is no longer accessible. We get a `NameError` when we try to access it outside the function.

The second concept to understand about variable scope is that if a local variable shares the same name as a global variable, any code inside the function is accessing the local variable. Any code outside is accessing the global variable. Try running the code below

```
message1 = "Global Variable (shares same
name as a local variable)"

def myFunction():
    message1 = "Local Variable (shares
same name as a global variable)"
    print("\nINSIDE THE FUNCTION")
    print (message1)

# Calling the function
myFunction()

# Printing message1 OUTSIDE the function
```

```
print ("\nOUTSIDE THE FUNCTION")
print (message1)
```

You'll get the output as follows:

```
INSIDE THE FUNCTION
Local Variable (shares same name as a
global variable)

OUTSIDE THE FUNCTION
Global Variable (shares same name as a
local variable)
```

When we print `message1` inside the function, it prints "`Local Variable (shares same name as a global variable)` " as it is printing the local variable. When we print it outside, it is accessing the global variable and hence prints "`Global Variable (shares same name as a local variable)`".

Importing Modules

Python comes with a large number of built-in functions. These functions are saved in files known as modules. To use the built-in codes in Python modules, we have to import them into our programs first. We do that by using the `import` keyword. There are three ways to do it.

The first way is to import the entire module by writing `import moduleName`.

For instance, to import the `random` module, we write `import random`.

To use the `randrange()` function in the `random` module, we write `random.randrange(1, 10)`.

If you find it too troublesome to write `random` each time you use the function, you can import the module by writing `import random as r` (where `r` is any name of your choice). Now to use the `randrange()` function, you simply write `r.randrange(1, 10)`.

The third way to import modules is to import specific functions from the module by writing `from moduleName import name1[, name2[, ... nameN]]`.

For instance, to import the `randrange()` function from the `random` module, we write `from random import randrange`. If we want to import more than one functions, we separate them with a comma. To import the `randrange()` and `randint()` functions, we write `from random import randrange, randint`. To use the function now, we do not have to use the dot notation anymore. Just write `randrange(1, 10)`.

Creating our Own Module

Besides importing built-in modules, we can also create our own modules. This is very useful if you have some functions that you want to reuse in other programming projects in future.

Creating a module is simple. Simply save the file with a .py extension and put it in the same folder as the Python file that you are going to import it from.

Suppose you want to use the `checkIfPrime()` function defined earlier in another Python script. Here's how you do it. First save the code above as `prime.py` on your desktop. `prime.py` should have the following code.

```
def checkIfPrime (numberToCheck):
    for x in range(2, numberToCheck):
        if (numberToCheck%x == 0):
            return False
    return True
```

Next, create another Python file and name it `useCheckIfPrime.py`. Save it on your desktop as well. `useCheckIfPrime.py` should have the following code.

```
import prime
answer = prime.checkIfPrime(13)
print (answer)
```

Now run `useCheckIfPrime.py`. You should get the output `True`. Simple as that.

However, suppose you want to store `prime.py` and `useCheckIfPrime.py` in different folders. You are going to have to add some codes to `useCheckIfPrime.py` to tell the Python interpreter where to find the module.

Say you created a folder named 'MyPythonModules' in your C drive to store `prime.py`. You need to add the following code to the top of your `useCheckIfPrime.py` file (before the line `import prime`).

```
import sys

if 'C:\\MyPythonModules' not in sys.path:
    sys.path.append('C:\\MyPythonModules')
```

`sys.path` refers to your Python's system path. This is the list of directories that Python goes through to search for modules and files. The code above appends the folder 'C:\MyPythonModules' to your system path.

Now you can put `prime.py` in C:\MyPythonModules and `checkIfPrime.py` in any other folder of your choice.

Chapter 8: Working with Files

Cool! We've come to the last chapter of the book before the project. In this chapter, we'll look at how to work with external files.

In Chapter 5 previously, we learned how to get input from users using the `input()` function. However, in some cases, getting users to enter data into our program may not be practical, especially if our program needs to work with large amounts of data. In cases like this, a more convenient way is to prepare the needed information as an external file and get our programs to read the information from the file. In this chapter, we are going to learn to do that. Ready?

Opening and Reading Text Files

The first type of file we are going to read from is a simple text file with multiple lines of text. To do that, let's first create a text file with the following lines.

Learn Python in One Day and Learn It Well
Python for Beginners with Hands-on Project
The only book you need to start coding in Python immediately
http://www.learncodingfast.com/python

Save this text file as `myfile.txt` to your desktop. Next, fire up IDLE and type the code below. Save this code as `fileOperation.py` to your desktop too.

```
f = open ('myfile.txt', 'r')
```

```
firstline = f.readline()
secondline = f.readline()
print (firstline)
print (secondline)

f.close()
```

The first line in the code opens the file. Before we can read from any file, we have to open it (just like you need to open this ebook on your kindle device or app to read it). The `open()` function does that and requires two parameters:

The first parameter is the path to the file. If you did not save `fileOperation.py` and `myfile.txt` in the same folder (desktop in this case), you need to replace `'myfile.txt'` with the actual path where you stored the text file. For instance, if you stored it in a folder named 'PythonFiles' in your C drive, you have to write `'C:\\PythonFiles\\myfile.txt'` (with double backslash \\).

The second parameter is the mode. This specifies how the file will be used. The commonly used modes are

'r' mode:
For reading only.

'w' mode:
For writing only.
If the specified file does not exist, it will be created.
If the specified file exists, any existing data on the file will be erased.

'a' mode:
For appending.
If the specified file does not exist, it will be created.
If the specified file exist, any data written to the file is automatically added to the end

'r+' mode:
For both reading and writing.

After opening the file, the next statement `firstline = f.readline()` reads the first line in the file and assigns it to the variable `firstline`.

Each time the `readline()` function is called, it reads a new line from the file. In our program, `readline()` was called twice. Hence the first two lines will be read. When you run the program, you'll get the output:

```
Learn Python in One Day and Learn It Well

Python for Beginners with Hands-on Project
```

You'll notice that a line break is inserted after each line. This is because the `readline()` function adds the `'\n'` characters to the end of each line. If you do not want the extra line between each line of text, you can do `print(firstline, end = '')`. This will remove the `'\n'` characters. After reading and printing the first two lines, the last sentence `f.close()` closes the file. You should always close the file once you finish reading it to free up any system resources.

Using a For Loop to Read Text Files

In addition to using the `readline()` method above to read a text file, we can also use a `for` loop. In fact, the `for` loop is a more elegant and efficient way to read text files. The following program shows how this is done.

```
f = open ('myfile.txt', 'r')

for line in f:
     print (line, end = '')

f.close()
```

The `for` loop loops through the text file line by line. When you run it, you'll get

```
Learn Python in One Day and Learn It Well
Python for Beginners with Hands-on Project
The only book you need to start coding in
Python immediately
http://www.learncodingfast.com/python
```

Writing to a Text File

Now that we've learned how to open and read a file, let's try writing to it. To do that, we'll use the 'a' (append) mode. You can also use the 'w' mode, but you'll erase all previous content in the file if the file already exists. Try running the following program.

```
f = open ('myfile.txt', 'a')
```

```
f.write ('\nThis sentence will be
appended.')
f.write ('\nPython is Fun!')

f.close()
```

Here we use the `write()` function to append the two sentences 'This sentence will be appended.' and 'Python is Fun!' to the file, each starting on a new line since we used the escape characters '\n'. You'll get

```
Learn Python in One Day and Learn It Well
Python for Beginners with Hands-on Project
The only book you need to start coding in
Python immediately
http://www.learncodingfast.com/python
This sentence will be appended.
Python is Fun!
```

Opening and Reading Text Files by Buffer Size

Sometimes, we may want to read a file by buffer size so that our program does not use too much memory resources. To do that, we can use the `read()` function (instead of the `readline()` function) which allows us to specify the buffer size we want. Try the following program:

```
inputFile = open ('myfile.txt', 'r')
outputFile = open ('myoutputfile.txt', 'w')

msg = inputFile.read(10)

while len(msg):
```

```
        outputFile.write(msg)
        msg = inputFile.read(10)

inputFile.close()
outputFile.close()
```

First, we open two files, the inputFile.txt and outputFile.txt files for reading and writing respectively.

Next, we use the statement msg = inputFile.read(10) and a while loop to loop through the file 10 bytes at a time. The value 10 in the parenthesis tells the read() function to only read 10 bytes. The while condition while len(msg): checks the length of the variable msg. As long as the length is not zero, the loop will run.

Within the while loop, the statement outputFile.write(msg) writes the message to the output file. After writing the message, the statement msg = inputFile.read(10) reads the next 10 bytes and keeps doing it until the entire file is read. When that happens, the program closes both files.

When you run the program, a new file myoutputfile.txt will be created. When you open the file, you'll notice that it has the same content as your input file myfile.txt. To prove that only 10 bytes is read at a time, you can change the line outputFile.write(msg) in the program to outputFile.write(msg + '\n'). Now run the program again. myoutputfile.txt now contains lines with at most 10 characters. Here's a segment of what you'll get.

```
Learn Pyth
on in One
Day and Le
arn It Wel
```

Opening, Reading and Writing Binary Files

Binary files refer to any file that contains non-text, such as image or video files. To work with binary files, we simply use the 'rb' or 'wb' mode. Copy a jpeg file onto your desktop and rename it `myimage.jpg`. Now edit the program above by changing the first two line lines

```
inputFile = open ('myfile.txt', 'r')
outputFile = open ('myoutputfile.txt', 'w')
```

to

```
inputFile = open ('myimage.jpg', 'rb')
outputFile = open ('myoutputimage.jpg',
'wb')
```

Make sure you also change the statement `outputFile.write(msg + '\n')` back to `outputFile.write(msg)`.

Run the new program. You should have an additional image file named `myoutputimage.jpg` on your desktop. When you open the image file, it should look exactly like `myimage.jpg`.

Deleting and Renaming Files

Two other useful functions we need to learn when working with files are the `remove()` and `rename()` functions. These functions are available in the `os` module and have to be imported before we can use them.

The `remove()` function deletes a file. The syntax is `remove(filename)`. For instance, to delete `myfile.txt`, we write `remove('myfile.txt')`.

The `rename()` function renames a file. The syntax is `rename (old name, new name)`. To rename `oldfile.txt` to `newfile.txt`, we write `rename('oldfile.txt', 'newfile.txt')`.

Project: Math and BODMAS

Congratulations! We've now covered enough fundamentals of Python (and programming in general) to start coding our first full program. In this chapter, we're going to code a program that tests our understanding of the BODMAS rule of arithmetic calculation. If you are unsure what BODMAS is, you can check out this site http://www.mathsisfun.com/operation-order-bodmas.html.

Our program will randomly set an arithmetic question for us to answer. If we get the answer wrong, the program will display the correct answer and ask if we want to try a new question. If we get it correct, the program will compliment us and ask if we want a new question. In addition, the program will keep track of our scores and save the scores in an external text file. After each question, we can key "-1" to terminate the program.

I've broken down the program into small exercises so that you can try coding the program yourself. Try the exercises before referring to the answers. Answers are provided in Appendix E or you can go to http://www.learncodingfast.com/python to download the Python files. I would strongly encourage you to download the source code as the formatting in Appendix E may result in the distortion of some indentation which makes the code difficult to read.

Remember, learning the Python syntax is easy but boring. Problem solving is where the fun lies. If you encounter difficulties when doing these exercises, try harder. This is where the reward is the greatest.

Ready? Let's go!

Part 1: myPythonFunctions.py

We will be writing two files for our programs. The first file is `myPythonFunctions.py` and the second is `mathGame.py`. Part 1 will focus on writing the code for `myPythonFunctions.py`.

To start, let's first create the file `myPythonFunctions.py`. We'll be defining three functions in this file.

Exercise 1: Importing Modules

We need to import two modules for `myPythonFunctions.py`: the `random` module and the `os` module.

We'll be using the `randint()` function from the `random` module. The `randint()` function generates a random integer within the range provided by us. We'll use that to generate numbers for our questions later.

From the `os` module, we'll be using the `remove()` and `rename()` functions.

Try importing these two modules.

Exercise 2: Getting the User's Score

Here we'll define our first function. Let's call it `getUserPoint()`. This function accepts one parameter, `userName`. It then opens the file `'userScores.txt'` in 'r' mode.

`userScores.txt` looks something like this:

```
Ann,  100
Benny,  102
Carol,  214
Darren,  129
```

Each line records the information of one user. The first value is the user's username and the second is the user's score.

Next, the function reads the file line by line using a `for` loop. Each line is then split using the `split()` function (refer to Appendix A for an example on using the `split()` function).

Let's store the results of the `split()` function in the list `content`.

Next, the function checks if any of the lines has the same username as the value that is passed in as the parameter. If there is, the function closes the file and returns the score beside that username. If there isn't, the function closes the file and returns the string '-1'.

Clear so far? Try coding the function.

Done?

Now we need to make some modifications to our code. When opening our file previously, we used the 'r' mode.

This helps to prevent any accidental changes to the file. However, when opening a file in 'r' mode, an `IOError` occurs if the file does not already exist. Hence when we run the program for the first time, we'll end up with an error since the file `userScores.txt` does not exist previously. To prevent this error, we can do either of the following:

Instead of opening the file in 'r' mode, we can open it in 'w' mode. When opening in 'w' mode, a new file will be created if the file does not exist previously. The risk with this method is we may accidentally write to the file, which results in all previous content being erased. However, since our program is a small program, we can check through our code carefully to prevent any accidental writing.

The second method is to use a `try, except` statement to handle the `IOError`. To do that, we need to put all our previous codes in the `try` block, then use `except IOError:` to handle the 'File not found' error. In the `except` block, we'll inform users that the file is not found and then proceed to create the file. We'll use the `open()` function with 'w' mode to create it. The difference here is we use the 'w' mode only when the file is not found. Since the file does not exist initially, there is no risk of erasing any previous content. After creating the file, close the file and return the string "-1".

You can choose either of the above methods to complete this exercise. The answer provided uses the second method. Once you are done, let's move on to Exercise 3.

Exercise 3: Updating the User's Score

In this exercise, we'll define another function called
`updateUserPoints()`, which takes in three parameters:
`newUser`, `userName` and `score`.

`newUser` can either be `True` or `False`. If `newUser` is
`True`, the function will open the file `userScores.txt` in
append mode and <u>append</u> the user's `userName` and
`score` to the file when he or she exits the game.

if `newUser` is `False`, the function will <u>update</u> the user's
score in the file. However, there is no function in Python (or
most programming languages for that matter) that allows
us to update a text file. We can only write or append to it,
but not update it.

Hence, we need to create a temporary file. This is a fairly
common practice in programming. Let's call this file
`userScores.tmp` and open it in 'w' mode. Now, we'll
need to loop through `userScore.txt` and copy the data
line by line to `userScores.tmp`. However, before
copying, we'll check if the `userName` on that line is the
same as the one provided as the parameter. If it is the
same, we'll change the score to the new score before
writing it to the temporary file.

For instance, if the parameters provided to the function are
`False`, 'Benny' and '158' (i.e.
`updateUserPoints(False, 'Benny', '158')`), the
table below shows the difference between the original
`userScores.txt` and the new `userScores.tmp`.

<u>userScores.txt</u>

```
Ann,  100
Benny,  102
Carol,  214
Darren, 129
```

<u>userScores.tmp</u>

```
Ann,  100
Benny,  158
Carol,  214
Darren, 129
```

After we finish writing to `userScore.tmp`, we'll close both files and delete `userScores.txt`. Finally, we'll rename `userScores.tmp` to `userScores.txt`.

Clear? Try coding it...

<u>Exercise 4: Generating the Questions</u>

We've now come to the most important part of the program, generating the mathematical questions. Ready?

To generate the questions, let's first declare three variables: two lists and one dictionary.

We shall name the two lists `operandList` and `operatorList`.

`operandList` should store five numbers, with 0 as their initial values. `operatorList` should store four strings, with ' ' as their initial values.

The dictionary consists of 4 pairs, with integers 1 to 4 as the dictionary keys, and "+", "-", "*", "**" as the data. Let's call this `operatorDict`.

[Exercise 4.1: Updating `operandList` with Random Numbers]

First we need to the replace the initial values of our `operandList` with random numbers generated by the `randint()` function.

The `randint()` takes in two parameters, `start` and `end`, and returns a random integer N such that `start` <= N <= `end`.

For instance, if `randint(1, 9)` is called, it'll randomly return an integer from the numbers 1, 2, 3, 4, 5, 6, 7, 8, 9.

To update our `operandList` variable with random numbers, we can do this one by one since `operandList` only has five members. We can write

```
operandList[0] = randint(1, 9)
operandList[1] = randint(1, 9)
operandList[2] = randint(1, 9)
operandList[3] = randint(1, 9)
operandList[4] = randint(1, 9)
```

Each time `randint(1, 9)` is called, it'll randomly return an integer from the numbers 1, 2, 3, 4, 5, 6, 7, 8, 9.

However, this is not the most elegant way of updating our `operandList`. Imagine how cumbersome it'll be if `operandList` has 1000 members. The better alternative is to use a `for` loop.

Try using a `for` loop to accomplish the same task.

Done? Great!

[Exercise 4.2: Updating `operatorList` with Mathematical Symbols]

Now that we have the numbers to operate on, we need to randomly generate the mathematical symbols (+, -, *, **) for our questions. To do that, we'll use the `randint()` function and the `operatorDict` dictionary.

`randint()` will generate the dictionary key, which will then be mapped to the correct operator using the `operatorDict` dictionary. For instance, to assign the symbol to `operatorList[0]`, we write

```
operatorList[0] = operatorDict[randint(1, 4)]
```

Similar to Exercise 4.1, you should use a `for` loop to complete this task. However, there is one problem that makes this exercise harder than Exercise 4.1.

Recall that in Python, ** stands for exponent (i.e. 2**3 = 2^3)?

The problem is, when we have two consecutive exponent operators in Python, such as 2**3**2, Python interprets it as 2**(3**2) instead of (2**3)**2. In the first case, the answer is 2 to the power of 9 (i.e. 2^9) which is 512. In the second case, the answer is 8 to the power of 2 (i.e. 8^2) which is 64. Hence when we present a question like 2**3**2, the user will get the answer wrong if he interprets it as (2**3)**2.

To prevent this problem, we're going to modify our code so that we do not get two consecutive ** signs. In other words, `operatorList = ['+', '+', '-', '**']` is fine but `operatorList = ['+', '-', '**', '**']` is not.

This exercise is the hardest among all the exercises. Try coming up with a solution to prevent two consecutive ** signs. Once you are done, we can proceed to Exercise 4.3.

Hint: If you are stuck, you can consider using an `if` statement within the `for` loop.

[Exercise 4.3: Generating a Mathematical Expression]

Now that we have our operators and operands, we are going to try to generate the mathematical expression as a string. This expression users the five numbers from our `operandList` and the four mathematical symbols from our `operatorList` to form a question.

We have to declare another variable called `questionString` and assign the mathematical expression to `questionString`. Examples of `questionString` include

6 – 2*3 – 2**1
4 + 5 – 2*6 + 1

$8 - 0*2 + 5 - 8$

Try to generate this expression yourself.

Hint: You can use a `for` loop to concatenate the individual substrings from `operandList` and `operatorList` to get the mathematical expression.

[Exercise 4.4: Evaluating the Result]

We should now have a mathematical expression as a string, assigned to the variable `questionString`. To evaluate the result of this expression, we're going to use a brilliant built-in function that comes with Python, `eval()`.

`eval()` interprets a string as a code and executes the code. For instance, if we write `eval("1+2+4")`, we'll get the number 7.

Hence to evaluate the result of our mathematical expression, we pass in `questionString` to the `eval()` function and assign the result to a new variable named `result`.

This exercise is pretty straight forward and can be completed in one step.

[Exercise 4.5: Interacting with the User]

Finally, we're going to interact with our user. In this exercise, we'll be doing a few things:

Step 1: Displaying the question to the user
Step 2: Prompting the user for an answer

Step 3: Evaluating the answer, displaying the appropriate message and returning the user's score.

For step 1, we need to use a built-in function for manipulating strings. As mentioned earlier, in Python, the ** symbol stands for exponent. That is, 2**3 = 8. However, to most users, ** has no meaning. Hence if we display a question as 2**3 + 8 -5, the user will likely be confused. To prevent that, we'll replace any ** symbol in `questionString` with the ^ symbol.

To do that, we'll use the built-in function `replace()`. Using it is pretty straightforward, just write `questionString = questionString.replace("**", "^")`. Now you can print the resulting expression to the user.

For step 2, you can use the `input()` function to accept user input.

For step 3, you should use an `if` statement to evaluate the answer and display the correct message. If the user gets it correct, we'll compliment the user and return the value 1. If the user gets it wrong, we'll display the correct answer and return the value 0.

Recall that the `input()` function returns user input as a string? Hence, when you compare the user's input with the correct answer (obtained in Exercise 4.4), you have to do some type casting to change the user input to an integer. When changing the user input to an integer, you should use a `try, except` statement to check if the user typed in a number. If the user typed in a string instead, the program should inform the user of the error and prompt the user to type in a number.

You can use a `while True` loop to keep prompting the user for a number as long as he/she fails to do so. Writing `while True` is equivalent to writing something like `while 1==1`. Since 1 is always equals to 1 (hence always `True`), the loop will run indefinitely.

Here's a suggestion on how you can use a `while True` loop for this exercise.

```
while True:
    try:
        cast user's answer to an integer
        and evaluate the answer
        return user score based on the
        answer
    except:
        print error message if casting
        fails
        prompt user to key in the answer
        again
```

The `while True` loop will keep looping since the `while` condition is always `True`. The loop will exit only when the `try` block executes correctly and reaches the `return` statement.

Try this exercise. Once you are done, we can proceed to Part 2 where we write the actual program.

Part 2: mathGame.py

Congratulations for completing Part 1 and welcome to Part 2. Part 2 is going to be a breeze as we'll mainly just be calling the functions we defined earlier.

Exercise 5: Writing the Main Program

First, let's enclose our main program in a `try, except` statement. We want to handle any unforeseen errors when running the main program.

We'll start by writing the code for the `try` block.

Firstly, we need to import the `myPythonFunctions` module. Next, let's prompt the user for his/her username and assign the value to the variable `userName`. Pass this variable as a parameter to the function `getUserScore()`.

`getUserScore()` will either return the score of the user or return '-1' (if the user is not found). Let's cast this result into an integer and assign it to the variable `userScore`.

Now, we need to set the value of another variable `newUser`. If the user is not found, `newUser = True`, else `newUser = False`. If `newUser = True`, we need to change `userScore` from -1 to 0.

The next part of our program involves a `while` loop. Specifically, our program will prompt for input from our user to determine if it should terminate the program or do something else.

Step 1:
You need to declare another variable `userChoice` and give it an initial value of 0.

Step 2:
Next, using a `while` loop, compare `userChoice` with a

string of your choice, say "-1". If `userChoice` is not the same as "-1", call the function `generateQuestion()` to generate a new question.

Step 3:
`generateQuestion()` will return the score that the user got for that question. Use this result to update the variable `userScore`.

Step 4:
Finally, in order to prevent an infinite loop, we need to use the `input()` function again <u>within</u> the while loop to accept user input and use it to update the value of `userChoice`.

Got that? Try coding it. Doing the actual coding will make everything clearer.

Finally, after the `while` loop terminates, the next step is to update the `userScores.txt` file. To do that, we simply call the `updateUserPoints()` function.

That's all for the `try` block. Now for the `except` block, we simply inform the user that an error has occurred and the program will exit.

That's it! Once you finish this step, you'll have a complete program, your first program in Python. Try running the program `mathGame.py`. Does it work as expected? Excited? I sure hope you are as excited about it as I am. :)

Challenge Yourself

We've come to the end of this chapter and hopefully you have successfully coded your first program. If you have problems completing any exercise, you can study the answers in Appendix E. You will learn a lot by studying other people's codes.

In this section, I have three additional exercises for you to challenge yourself.

Challenge Exercise 1

In the program that we've coded so far, I've avoided using the division operator. Can you modify the program so that it'll generate questions with the division sign too? How would you check the user's answer against the correct answer?

Hint: Check out the `round()` function.

Challenge Exercise 2

Sometimes, the question generated may result in an answer that is very large or very small. For instance, the question 6*(8^9/1)^3 will give the answer 1450710985375550096474112.

It is very inconvenient for users to calculate and key in such a large number. Hence, we want to avoid answers that are too big or small. Can you modify the program to prevent questions that result in answers greater than 50 000 or smaller than -50000?

Challenge Exercise 3

The last challenge exercise is the most difficult.

So far, brackets are missing in the questions generated. Can you modify the program so that the questions use brackets too? An example of a question will be 2 + (3*7 -1) + 5.

Have fun with these exercises. The suggested solution is provided in Appendix E.

Thank You

We've come to the end of the book. Thank you for reading this book and I hope you have enjoyed the book. More importantly, I sincerely hope the book has helped you master the fundamentals of Python programming.

I know you could have picked from a dozen of books on Python Programming, but you took a chance with this book. Thank you once again for downloading this book and reading all the way to the end. Please do try the exercises and challenges. You'll learn a lot by doing.

Now I'd like to ask for a "small" favor. Could you please take a few minutes or two to leave a review for this book on Amazon?

To leave a review, simply search for "Learn Python in One Day and Learn It Well" on Amazon. Once you are on the book's product page, click on the link x customer reviews.

Then click on Create Your Own Review

Customer Reviews
Learn Python in One Day and Learn It Well: Python for Beginners with Hands-on P
immediately

	2 Reviews	
5 star:	▓▓▓▓▓	(2)
4 star:		(0)
3 star:		(0)
2 star:		(0)
1 star:		(0)

Average Customer Review
★★★★★ (2 customer reviews)

Share your thoughts with other customers

Create your own review

This feedback will help me tremendously and will help me continue to write more guides on programming. If you like the book or have any suggestions for improvement, please let me know. I will be deeply grateful. :)

Last but not least, remember you can download the source code for the project and the appendices at http://www.learncodingfast.com/python.

You can also contact me at jamie@learncodingfast.com.

Appendix A: Working With Strings

Note: The notation [start, [end]] means *start* and *end* are optional parameters. If only one number is provided as the parameter, it is taken to be *start*.

\# marks the start of a comment
''' marks the start and end of a multiline comment
The actual code is in `monotype` font.
=> marks the start of the output

count (sub, [start, [end]])

Return the number of times the substring *sub* appears in the string.
This function is case-sensitive.

[Example]

\# In the examples below, 's' occurs at index 3, 6 and 10

```
# count the entire string
'This is a string'.count('s')
=> 3
```

```
# count from index 4 to end of string
'This is a string'.count('s', 4)
=> 2
```

```
# count from index 4 to 10-1
'This is a string'.count('s', 4, 10 )
=> 1
```

```
# count 'T'. There's only 1 'T' as the function is case sensitive.
'This is a string'.count('T')
=> 1
```

---

endswith (suffix, [start, [end]])

Return True if the string ends with the specified *suffix*,
otherwise return False.
suffix can also be a tuple of suffixes to look for.
This function is case-sensitive.

[Example]

'man' occurs at index 4 to 6

check the entire string
```
'Postman'.endswith('man')
```
=> True

check from index 3 to end of string
```
'Postman'.endswith('man', 3)
```
=> True

check from index 2 to 6-1
```
'Postman'.endswith('man', 2, 6)
```
=> False

check from index 2 to 7-1
```
'Postman'.endswith('man', 2, 7)
```
=> True

Using a tuple of suffixes (check from index 2 to 6-1)
```
'Postman'.endswith(('man', 'ma'), 2, 6)
```
=> True

find/index (sub, [start, [end]])

Return the index in the string where the first occurrence of
the substring *sub* is found.
find() returns -1 if *sub* is not found.
index() returns ValueError is *sub* is not found.
This function is case-sensitive.

[Example]

```
# check the entire string
'This is a string'.find('s')
=> 3

# check from index 4 to end of string
'This is a string'.find('s', 4)
=> 6

# check from index 7 to 11-1
'This is a string'.find('s', 7,11 )
=> 10

# Sub is not found
'This is a string'.find('p')
=> -1

'This is a string'.index('p')
=> ValueError
```

isalnum()

Return true if all characters in the string are alphanumeric and there is at least one character, false otherwise. Alphanumeric does not include whitespaces.

[Example]

```
'abcd1234'.isalnum()
=> True

'a b c d 1 2 3 4'.isalnum()
=> False

'abcd'.isalnum()
=> True
```

```
'1234'.isalnum()
```
=> True

isalpha()

Return true if all characters in the string are alphabetic and there is at least one character, false otherwise.

[Example]

```
'abcd'.isalpha()
```
=> True

```
'abcd1234'.isalpha()
```
=> False

```
'1234'.isalpha()
```
=> False

```
'a b c'.isalpha()
```
=> False

isdigit()

Return true if all characters in the string are digits and there is at least one character, false otherwise.

[Example]

```
'1234'.isdigit()
```
=> True

```
'abcd1234'.isdigit()
```
=> False

```
'abcd'.isdigit()
```
=> False

```
'1 2 3 4'.isdigit()
```
=> False

islower()

Return true if all cased characters in the string are lowercase and there is at least one cased character, false otherwise.

[Example]

```
'abcd'.islower()
```
=> True

```
'Abcd'.islower()
```
=> False

```
'ABCD'.islower()
```
=> False

isspace()

Return true if there are only whitespace characters in the string and there is at least one character, false otherwise.

[Example]

```
' '.isspace()
```
=> True

```
'a b'.isspace()
```
=> False

istitle()

Return true if the string is a titlecased string and there is at least one character

[Example]

```
'This Is A String'.istitle()
=> True

'This is a string'.istitle()
=> False
```

isupper()

Return true if all cased characters in the string are uppercase and there is at least one cased character, false otherwise.

[Example]

```
'ABCD'.isupper()
=> True

'Abcd'.isupper()
=> False

'abcd'.isupper()
=> False
```

join()

Return a string in which the parameter provided is joined by a separator.

[Example]

```
sep = '-'
myTuple = ('a', 'b', 'c')
myList = ['d', 'e', 'f']
myString = "Hello World"

sep.join(myTuple)
```
=> 'a-b-c'

```
sep.join(myTuple)
```
=> 'd-e-f'

```
sep.join(myString)
```
=> 'H-e-l-l-o- -W-o-r-l-d"

lower()

Return a copy of the string converted to lowercase.

[Example]

```
'Hello Python'.lower()
```
=> 'hello python'

replace(old, new[, count])

Return a copy of the string with all occurrences of
substring old replaced by new.
count is optional. If given, only the first count occurrences
are replaced.
This function is case-sensitive.

[Example]

```
# Replace all occurences
'This is a string'.replace('s', 'p')
```

=> 'Thip ip a ptring'

Replace first 2 occurences
```
'This is a string'.replace('s', 'p', 2)
```
=> 'Thip ip a string'

split([sep [,maxsplit]])

Return a list of the words in the string, using *sep* as the delimiter string.
sep and *maxsplit* are optional.
If *sep* is not given, whitespace is used as the delimiter.
If *maxsplit* is given, at most *maxsplit* splits are done.
This function is case-sensitive.

[Example]

""

Split using comma as the delimiter
Notice that there's a space before the words 'is', 'a' and 'string' in the output.
""
```
'This, is, a, string'.split(',')
```
=> ['This', ' is', ' a', ' string']

Split using whitespace as delimiter
```
'This is a string'.split()
```
=> ['This', 'is', 'a', 'string']

Only do 2 splits
```
'This, is, a, string'.split(',' 2)
```
=> ['This', ' is', ' a, string']

splitlines ([keepends])

Return a list of the lines in the string, breaking at line boundaries.

Line breaks are not included in the resulting list unless *keepends* is given and true.

[Example]

```
# Split lines separated by \n
'This is the first line.\nThis is the
second line'.splitlines()
=> ['This is the first line.', 'This is the second line.']
```

```
# Split multi line string (e.g. string that uses the ''' mark)
'''This is the first line.
This is the second line.'''.splitlines()
=> ['This is the first line.', 'This is the second line.']
```

```
# Split and keep line breaks
'This is the first line.\nThis is the
second line.'.splitlines(True)
=> ['This is the first line.\n', 'This is the second line.']
```

```
'''This is the first line.
This is the second
line.'''.splitlines(True)
=> ['This is the first line.\n', 'This is the second line.']
```

startswith (prefix[, start[, end]])

Return True if string starts with the prefix, otherwise return False.
prefix can also be a tuple of prefixes to look for.
This function is case-sensitive.

[Example]

```
# 'Post' occurs at index 0 to 3
```

```
# check the entire string
```

```
'Postman'.startswith('Post')
```
=> True

```
# check from index 3 to end of string
'Postman'.startswith('Post', 3)
```
=> False

```
# check from index 2 to 6-1
'Postman'.startswith('Post', 2, 6)
```
=> False

```
# check from index 2 to 6-1
'Postman'.startswith('stm', 2, 6)
```
=> True

```
# Using a tuple of prefixes (check from index 3 to end of
string)
'Postman'.startswith(('Post', 'tma'), 3)
```
=> True

strip ([chars])

Return a copy of the string with the leading and trailing characters *char* removed.
If *char* is not provided, whitespaces will be removed.
This function is case-sensitive.

[Example]

```
# Strip whitespaces
'    This is a string    '.strip()
```
=> 'This is a string'

```
# Strip 's'. Nothing is removed since 's' is not at the start or
end of the string
'This is a string'.strip('s')
```
=> 'This is a string'

```
print (len(myTuple))
=> 4
```

Addition Operator: +

Concatenate Tuples

[Example]

```
myTuple = ('a', 'b', 'c', 'd')
print (myTuple + ('e', 'f'))
=> ('a', 'b', 'c', 'd', 'e', 'f')

print (myTuple)
=> ('a', 'b', 'c', 'd')
```

Multiplication Operator: *

Duplicate a tuple and concatenate it to the end of the tuple

[Example]

```
myTuple = ('a', 'b', 'c', 'd')
print (myTuple*3)
=> ('a', 'b', 'c', 'd', 'a', 'b', 'c', 'd', 'a', 'b', 'c', 'd')

print (myTuple)
=> ('a', 'b', 'c', 'd')
```

Note: The + and * symbols do not modify the tuple. The tuple stays as ['a', 'b', 'c', 'd'] in both cases.

Appendix D: Working With Dictionaries

=> marks the start of the output

clear( )

Removes all elements of the dictionary, returning an empty dictionary

[Example]

```
dic1 = {1: 'one', 2: 'two'}
print (dic1)
=> {1: 'one', 2: 'two'}

dic1.clear()
print (dic1)
=> {}
```

del

Delete the entire dictionary

[Example]

```
dic1 = {1: 'one', 2: 'two'}
del dic1
print (dic1)
=> NameError: name 'dic1' is not defined
```

get( )

Returns a value for the given key.
If the key is not found, it'll return the keyword None.